I0201560

ANIMALS IN THE CITY

Rats

Ava Podmorow

Explore other books at:
WWW.ENGAGEBOOKS.COM

VANCOUVER, B.C.

WWW.ENGAGEBOOKS.COM

Rats: Level Pre-1
Animals in the City
Podmorow, Ava 2004 –
Text © 2022 Engage Books
Design © 2022 Engage Books

Edited by: A.R. Roumanis
and Sarah Harvey

Text set in Epilogue

FIRST EDITION / FIRST PRINTING

All rights reserved. No part of this book may be stored in a retrieval system, reproduced or transmitted in any form or by any other means without written permission from the publisher or a licence from the Canadian Copyright Licensing Agency. Critics and reviewers may quote brief passages in connection with a review or critical article in any media.

Every reasonable effort has been made to contact the copyright holders of all material reproduced in this book.

LIBRARY AND ARCHIVES CANADA CATALOGUING IN PUBLICATION

Title: Rats / Ava Podmorow
Names: Podmorow, Ava, author.
Description: Series statement: Animals in the city
Engaging readers: level pre-1, beginner.

Identifiers: Canadiana (print) 20220406723 | Canadiana (ebook) 20220406731
ISBN 978-1-77476-768-9 (hardcover)
ISBN 978-1-77476-769-6 (softcover)
ISBN 978-1-77476-770-2 (epub)
ISBN 978-1-77476-771-9 (pdf)

Subjects:
LCSH: Readers (Elementary)
LCSH: Readers—Rats.
LCGFT: Readers (Publications)

Classification: LCC PE1119.2 .P644 2022 | DDC J428.6/2—DC23

This project has been made possible in part
by the Government of Canada.

Canada

Rats are always hungry!

3

Rats live
in cities.

It is easy to find food and places to sleep.

Rats love to
eat meat.

They eat a lot of garbage too.

Rats are often found near garbage, but they hate to be dirty.

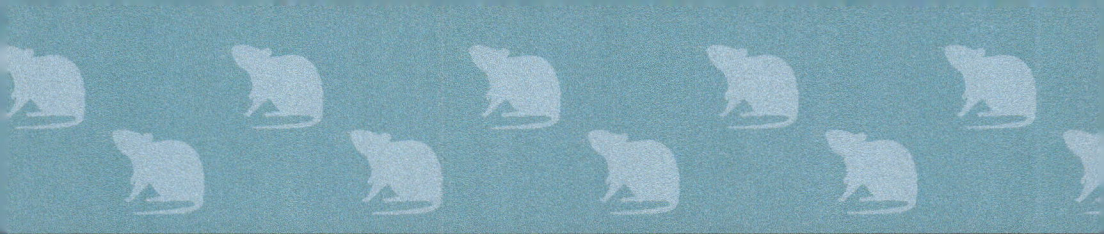

They clean
themselves often.

There are many different kinds of rats.

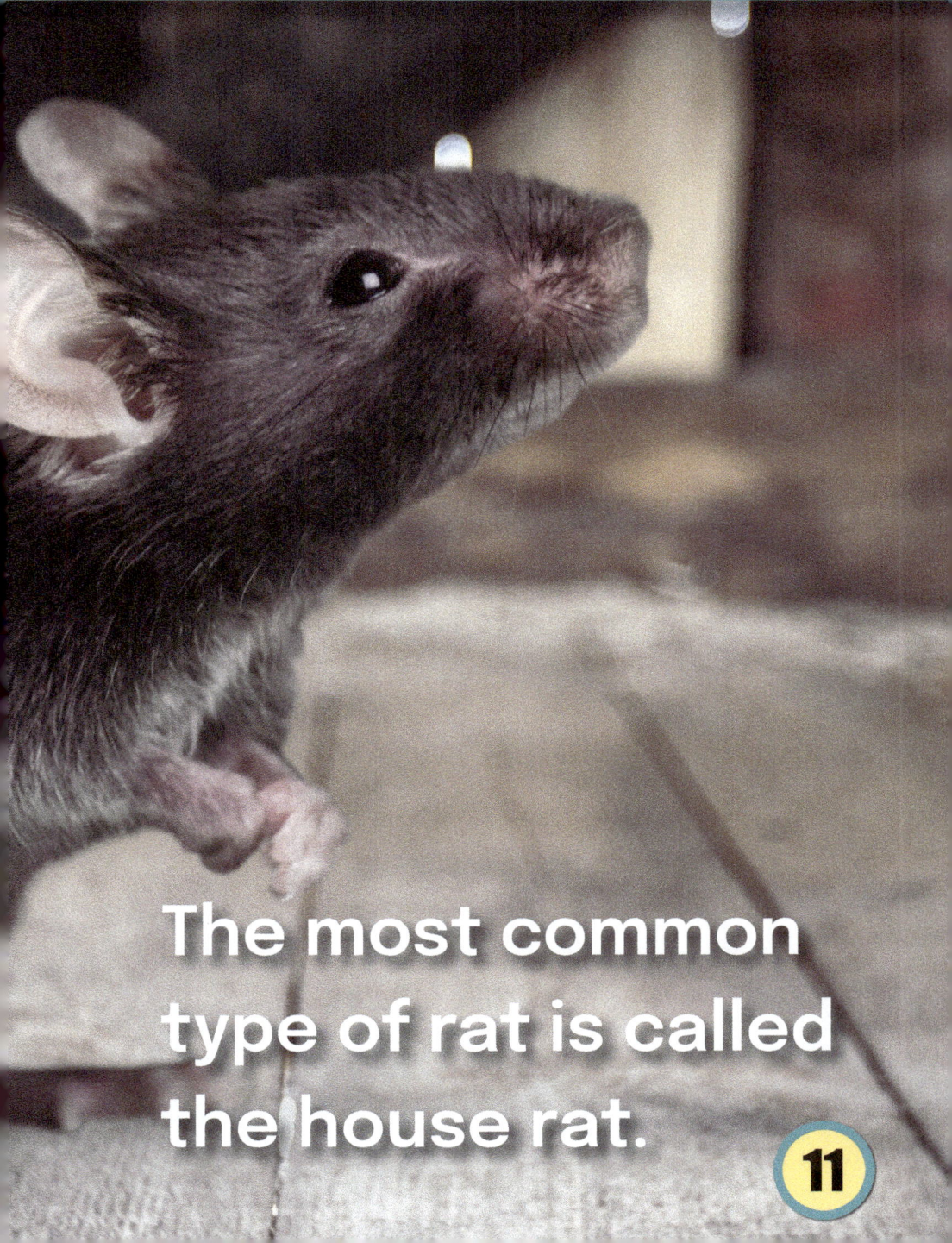

The most common type of rat is called the house rat.

It is rare to find
one rat on its own.

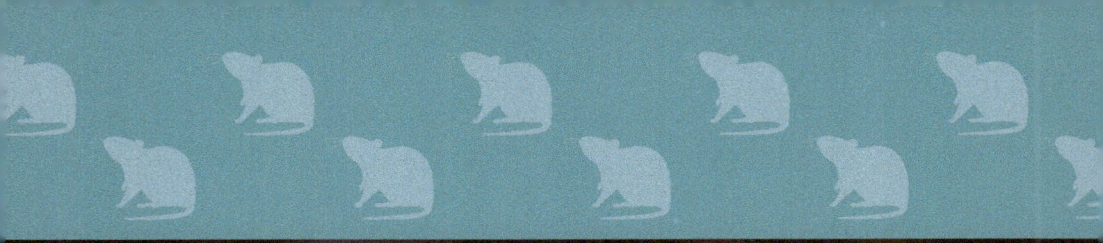

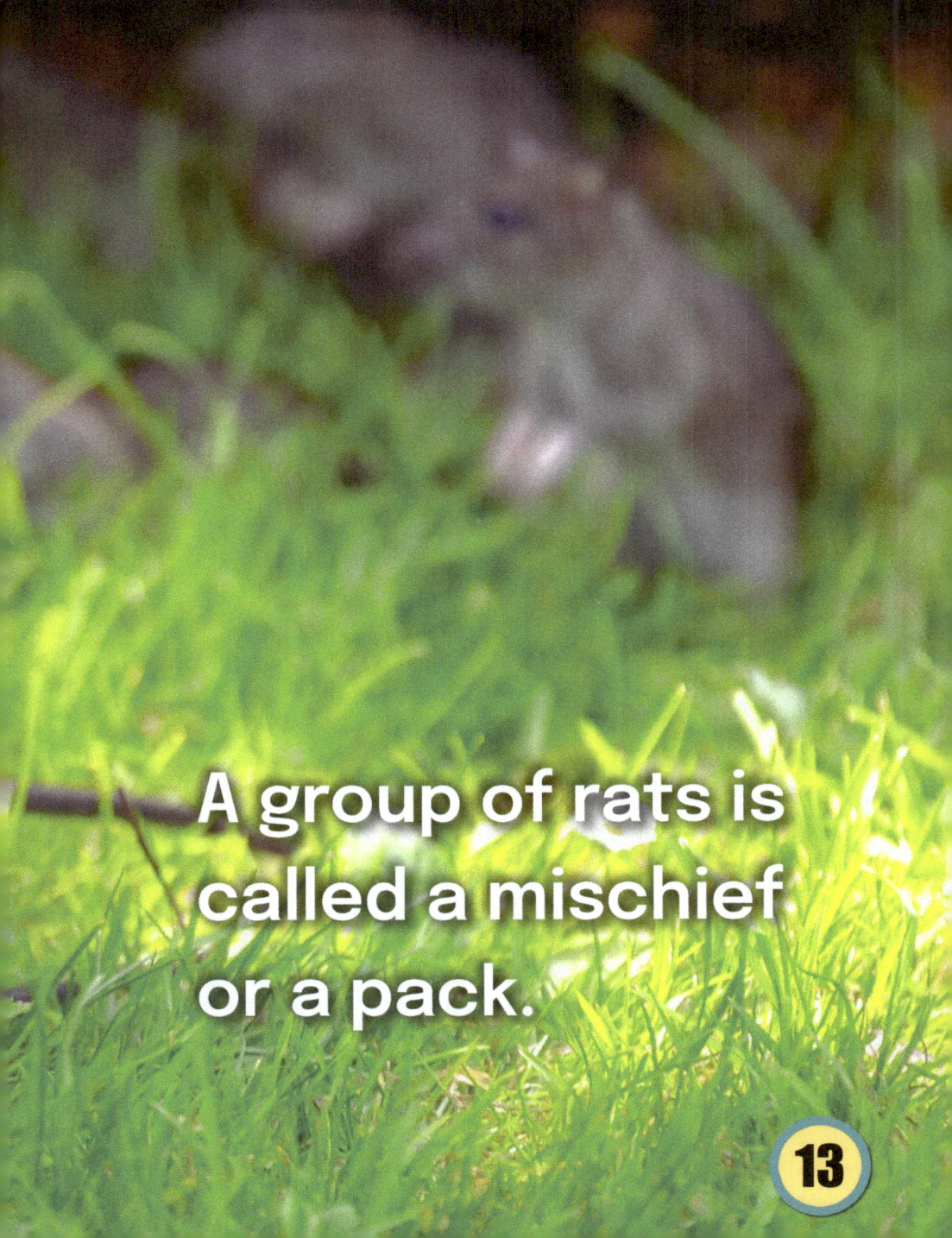

A group of rats is called a mischief or a pack.

Rats have short hair, long tails, and whiskers. Their eyes are large.

Hair

Long Tail

Eyes

Whiskers

Rats can only see things that are very close to them.

Things that are far away are blurry.

17

Rats can hear
better than humans.

New noises
scare them.

Female rats can have babies six times a year.

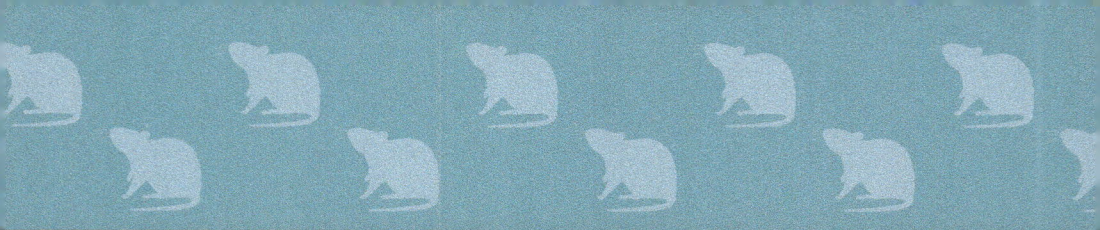

The teeth on
a rat never
stop growing!

Chewing
keeps their
teeth short.

Some people keep rats as pets.

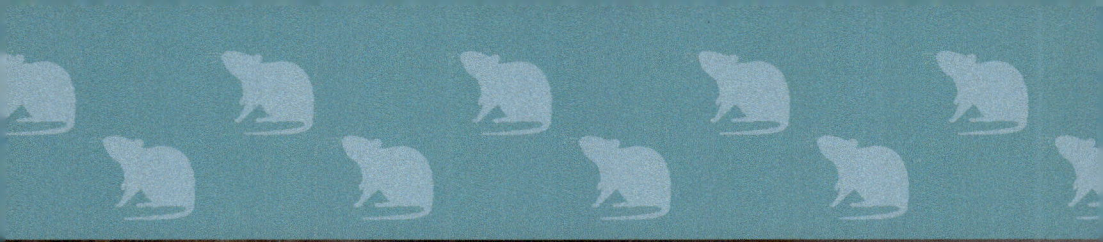

Most people think they are pests.

25

Rats are great swimmers.

They can hold their breath underwater a long time.

27

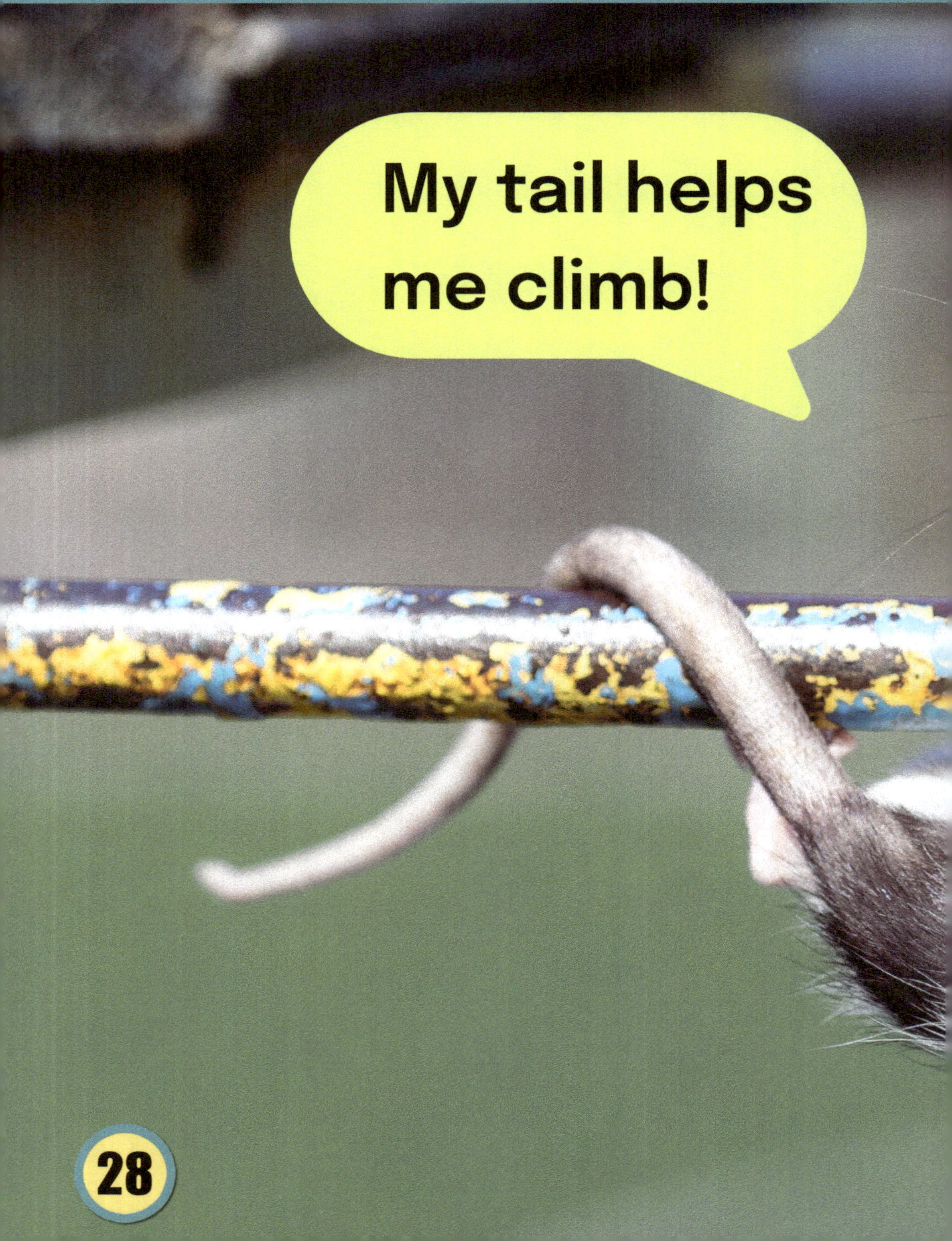
My tail helps me climb!

Explore other books in the Animals In The City series.

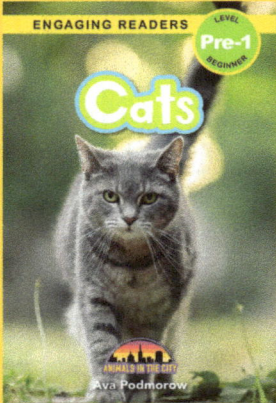

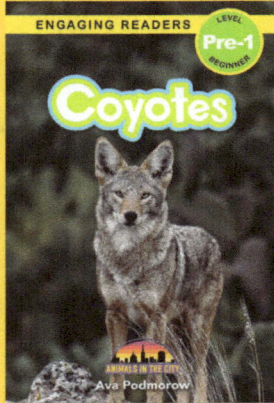

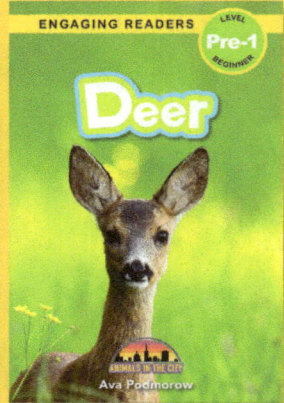

ENGAGING READERS — LEVEL Pre-1 BEGINNER
Cats
Ava Podmorow

ENGAGING READERS — LEVEL Pre-1 BEGINNER
Coyotes
Ava Podmorow

ENGAGING READERS — LEVEL Pre-1 BEGINNER
Deer
Ava Podmorow

ENGAGING READERS — LEVEL Pre-1 BEGINNER
Owls
Ava Podmorow

ENGAGING READERS — LEVEL Pre-1 BEGINNER
Pigeons
Ava Podmorow

ENGAGING READERS — LEVEL Pre-1 BEGINNER
Rabbits
Ava Podmorow

ENGAGING READERS — LEVEL Pre-1 BEGINNER
Raccoons
Sarah Harvey

ENGAGING READERS — LEVEL Pre-1 BEGINNER
Rats
Ava Podmorow

ENGAGING READERS — LEVEL Pre-1 BEGINNER
Skunks
Ava Podmorow

Visit www.engagebooks.com/readers

Explore level 1 readers with the Animals That Make a Difference series.

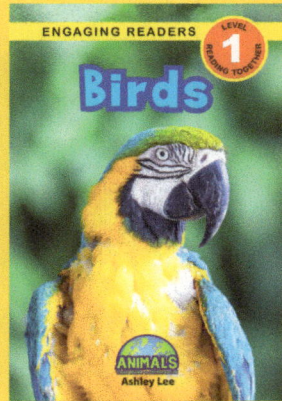

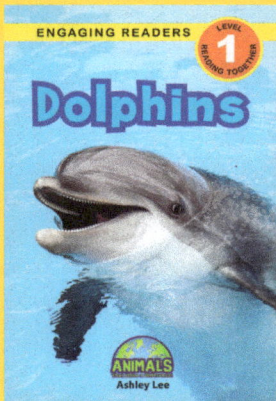

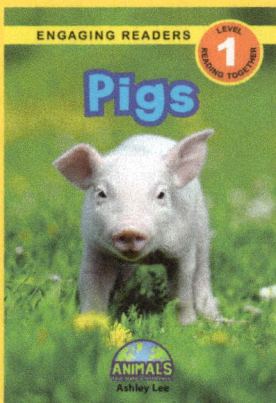

ENGAGING READERS — LEVEL 1 READING TOGETHER

Bees
Jared Siemens
ANIMALS

Bats
Ashley Lee
ANIMALS

Birds
Ashley Lee
ANIMALS

Dolphins
Ashley Lee
ANIMALS

Horses
Ashley Lee
ANIMALS

Ladybugs
Ashley Lee
ANIMALS

Pigs
Ashley Lee
ANIMALS

Sharks
Ashley Lee
ANIMALS

Squirrels
Ashley Lee
ANIMALS

Visit www.engagebooks.com/readers

www.ingramcontent.com/pod-product-compliance
Lightning Source LLC
Chambersburg PA
CBHW051239020426
42331CB00016B/3451